The Vanguard

Landell Bartlett

Alpha Editions

This edition published in 2024

ISBN : 9789362925091

Design and Setting By
Alpha Editions
www.alphaedis.com
Email - info@alphaedis.com

As per information held with us this book is in Public Domain.
This book is a reproduction of an important historical work. Alpha Editions uses the best technology to reproduce historical work in the same manner it was first published to preserve its original nature. Any marks or number seen are left intentionally to preserve its true form.

The lights had now reached their maximum, giving the huge room the effect of being flooded by intensely bright moonlight. Behind me, and on all sides, stood scores of these creatures, similar in appearance to the Field General on the throne. They stood motionless, regarding me stolidly with their smoldering, beady eyes.... Finally Oomlag turned to me: "The Field General wants to ask you a few questions," he said, stepping to one side.

The VANGUARD of VENUS

By LANDELL BARTLETT

(Extract from letter dated February 16, 1927, from Oliver Robertson, banker of Calcutta, India, to J. B. Cardigan, President of Cardigan Press Service, Inc.)

. . . . . we got into a pretty hot argument over it, too. Of course, I thought Morrison was kidding me at first; but he kept insisting that Murdock wouldn't have done such a thing if he really hadn't meant it for the truth.

I told him that Murdock had probably had his little secret hobby of fiction-writing unknown to any of his friends, that he had thought up this story for his own entertainment, and had taken this means of making it "plausible." I admit I don't understand why he should want to do such a thing, but I think you will agree with me that at least it is very clever. You can never tell what these serious-minded, middle-aged bachelors are going to do next. I was really quite exasperated at Morrison for believing this story. He knew poor Stanley better than I, it is true; but as joint executor of the estate, I insisted that if it were to be published at all, it should be as fiction, pure and simple. Then, if anyone wants to believe it, let him go to it.

Morrison argued that the notarial seal and the definite instructions on the envelope showed Murdock meant business—that he wasn't the kind to clutter up a strong box with junk. He reminded me that Murdock had chucked a fine position in the United States to come to India on a smaller salary and in a technically inferior rating, which was a fair indication of the truth of his story. Murdock was unimaginative as far as I know, but this story seems to indicate otherwise. He was a splendid chap, sober and industrious. He was the only one killed in that wreck of the Central of India at Coomptah ten days ago . . .

Knowing you are in touch with publishers that can handle this sort of thing, I have taken the liberty of sending you Murdock's document herewith, together with the envelope in which it was found. You will note that the instructions on the envelope indicate that it was to be opened only in the event of Murdock's death, by his executors, or by himself, on June 21, 1931. If you can dispose of this material for profit, I certainly will appreciate it.

N. B.—Touched up a bit, it might make good reading—in fact, I think it is deucedly interesting as it stands.

Let me know as soon as possible, old man, what you think of this and what disposition you want to make of it. I'll appreciate it very much if you can find a publisher, for it was Stanley's wish . . .

> Your old, hard-headed cousin,
>
> OLIVER ROBERTSON.

(Stanley Murdock's document, enclosed with the above letter, printed just as he himself wrote it. Pursuant to Mr. Robertson's instructions, and to prevent uneasiness among the credulous, the public is warned that the story is undoubtedly fiction.)

September 18, 1923.
47 Victoria Drive, Rajput Gardens,
Calcutta, India,

TO WHOM THIS MAY CONCERN:

In accordance with instructions I have filed with the officials of the Calcutta Traders' Bank, this document, which is to be read by my executors in the event of my death before June 21, 1931, or by myself on that date in the presence of three officers of the above bank. The reason for this I shall explain as clearly as possible.

An experience befell me while doing geological work in the United States of America that has profoundly altered my life, and by the year 1931, will alter the lives of every human being in the world. This statement, startling and unbelievable as it may sound, is nevertheless the truth, and is the reason I am writing, or you are reading this. And I am taking the only course consistent with my own welfare in giving this message to the public so that it may have even a slight chance of credence.

So preposterous will be found the contents of this document that such fact alone will largely explain my method of procedure. I want this message to be read, to be believed, and to be acted on. Had I told anybody of my experience at the time it happened, I would simply have been the laughing stock of my friends. Insisting on the truth of the story might have been cause for investigation as to my sanity, and the loss of my position if not of my liberty. It was utterly out of the question to even think of telling anyone what I saw. I had absolutely no proof, and could not then, let alone now, produce any evidence to back up my statements. Only time will prove that I am right, and that will be not later than August 21, 1931. There is a remote chance that the catastrophe will occur sooner, but knowing what I do, I believe that it will transpire on that exact date. So you can see what an awkward position I am in—a prophet—foretelling happenings years ahead, to the very day, to a skeptical world bound by the age-old dictum of common sense, to laugh him to scorn.

This, then, is the reason I have made the safeguards for reading this manuscript. The message being so vital to the world, I have deposited copies in the largest banks in Bombay and Madras. These documents are to be mailed to me on June 21, 1931, or in case I die, may be obtained by my executors any time before that date. Thus I will avoid practically eight years of derision with attendant loss of position and probable confinement for mental instability. At the same time, my warning is in no danger of being lost, and will be given to the world in time to do some possible good. If I am alive on June 21, 1931, I shall give my experience to the world on that date, allowing two months for those who heed it to escape a terrible fate. The reason I resigned my position in the United States and am now in India will be disclosed in the narrative.

IT was in January, 1923, that I met with this staggering experience. At that time I was employed by the Southwestern Syndicate as chief geologist for the Arizona-New Mexico district. I had been with them almost fifteen years, going to them from the Concord Company, with whom I had been associated since my graduation from the Massachusetts Institute of Technology. Both of these companies, if I can judge by the testimonials they so generously gave me on my resignation, rated me very highly, and were reluctant to part with my services. I mention this not in self-praise, but to show that I have always had a reputation for honesty and efficient work. And I sincerely hope that this reputation will sustain me when I say that what I am about to relate here is the absolute truth.

On January 14, 1923, Olin Gilfillan (my most trusted field lieutenant and a brilliant, hard-working man) and I set out on horseback from Lovington, New Mexico, and headed toward the Mescalero Ridge. We had with us a couple of pack mules bearing camping equipment and grub for a week. It was our intention to scout the southeast part of the Ridge, and report certain findings to the company. I shall not here relate any technical description of our route, inasmuch as my complete report is on file with the company in their Chicago office.

We left Lovington in the morning, and after a leisurely trip with a few stops for "sighting," made camp in a little arroyo leading up to the Ridge. The day had been wonderfully clear, and in the early twilight I worked on my notes while Olin built a small fire of cedar and mesquite and prepared the coffee and bacon. After supper we lit our pipes and talked over various things until about nine, when we crawled into our sleeping bags.

It was some time before I dropped off, as there were several problems connected with the trip that I kept reviewing in my mind. I could hear Olin's steady breathing, and envied him his ability to sleep soundly under any conditions. Up from the east swam a large, perfect full moon, flooding our camp in the little arroyo with its cold light. From far away came the indistinct, silly yapping of a couple of coyotes, and I could hear the horses stirring uneasily. Finally I fell asleep, and it seemed as though I had hardly closed my eyes when something—perhaps a sound, or maybe a premonition of something wrong—caused me to become wide awake. I sat up and, noticing that the moon was now overhead, looked at my wrist watch. It was almost one o'clock.

There seemed to be nothing amiss. Olin was snoring peacefully, the coyotes were no longer serenading the moon, only a little breeze was moving the tops of the mesquite brushes. I glanced over to where the horses had been tethered, and saw that they were very restive. Thinking that perhaps some coyote was skulking about our camp, I crawled out of my sleeping bag, took my rifle, and went over to where the horses were trembling and straining at their tethers. They were apparently scared at something immediately in front of them, as they both gazed with bulging eyes in the same direction. Aside from a large rock and a few straggling sotol plants, I could see nothing to cause their fear. Thinking that perhaps, some creature had hidden behind the rock, I made my way in a wide circle around it, but there was nothing I could see to explain the horses' fright. I went to them and stroked their noses; this calmed them somewhat, but they continued to gaze fearfully at the rock.

IT came over me like a flash that I had not noticed that rock when we made camp—in fact, being now fully wide awake, I recalled that there was no large rock of any kind near our camp. I blinked my eyes and pinched myself to see if I was really awake. Could I have been mistaken about my first impression of our camp site, and have overlooked an object as large as that rock? My work has always called for keen observation, and it was absurd to think that if a fairly sizable boulder had been in sight, especially all by itself as this one was, I would have failed to note it. Yet there it was, gleaming dully in the moonlight, apparently firmly imbedded in the ground. But it *couldn't* (I reasoned) have been there when we first arrived. Imagine two geologists failing to see a rock of that size! How in the world could it have gotten there? Was it placed there by someone during the night, while we slept? And if so, why? But I had not noticed any footprints around it. It was obvious that it could not have rolled from anywhere. It had not been there four hours ago, it had not been carried, it had not rolled ...

In all my experiences in out-of-the-way, God-forsaken places, I have never known fear. I have been shot at by Mexicans, held up by thugs, even bitten by a rattlesnake—but nothing has ever made me afraid. Not even intense shell fire on the Western Front, where I had served the last month of the war as an infantry captain in the 8th Division, ever made me aware of danger. I was cited once by the French government for bravery, but I take no credit for that. It is simply my make-up—I have no "nerves." But now—this inexplicable rock appearing from nowhere—the very obvious fear it instilled in the horses—

My first impulse was to waken Olin and tell him of this startling phenomenon. The remote possibility that I might be mistaken, and had for some reason failed to notice this rock, due to my absorption in my note making, deterred me. How Olin would laugh at me if I roused him because of some foolish fancy about an innocent boulder that had been there all the time. He would never get done guying the life out of me. But I was positive that it had not been there when we made camp.

I was debating whether to investigate the rock and prove once for all there was no cause for alarm, or arouse Olin and get his opinion, when the rock was suddenly thrown back and I could see that it was only a hollow camouflage over a hole in the ground. Before I could cry out, I was seized from behind and strong hands had placed a gag in my mouth and a bandage over my eyes. I attempted to struggle, but my efforts were useless. It was as though my arms and legs were held in a powerful vise. Something sweetish that may have been chloroform was held over my nose, and before I lost consciousness I heard the squeal of a horse and the pounding of his hoofs as he broke from his tether and ran. There was no sound of any kind from my captors. I was dimly aware of being carried in powerful arms and laid upon some smooth surface that seemed to sink beneath me as darkness pressed upon me and I knew no more.

HOW long it was before I regained consciousness I do not know. I seemed to hear a sort of droning sound, like the faraway purr of an aeroplane motor. For a stupefied instant I believed I was again in my sleeping bag, awakening from a bad dream. Then the recollection of the hollow rock and my silent capture by strong hands seizing me swiftly from behind, the thundering hoofs of the frightened horse, came over me with sickening vividness. Cautiously I moved my arms and legs, and found that they were not bound. Neither was there a gag in my mouth or a bandage over my eyes. It was too dark to see anything of my surroundings, but I could feel that I was lying on a gently sloping, smooth, cold stone floor. I got unsteadily to my feet and carefully extended my hands above my head. Though I reached upward as far as I could, I could touch nothing. I got down on my knees and groped around, crawling several feet in every direction, and encountered no obstacle of any kind—only the smooth, dry stone that was the floor of my strange prison.

There was no way of telling the dimensions of the room or cave in which I had been deserted by my mysterious captors. Utter darkness enveloped me like a heavy blanket. After several minutes of futile crawling around, I realized that I must be in the middle of some tremendous room, and that it was a waste of time trying to find a wall or outlet. My captors evidently knew that this Stygian blackness would effectually bar my escape, even if there were a way out, and that was undoubtedly the reason I was unbound. Nothing I could do would help in any way, so I might just as well await developments calmly. I stretched myself full length on the stone floor and tried to puzzle out the reason for my terrible predicament.

That I had been kidnapped by bandits and removed to some cavern to await the payment of ransom seemed the most plausible solution. I wondered if they had seized Olin Gilfillan also. If so, why were we not together? Thinking he might be somewhere nearby, I shouted his name aloud. Only the hollow, booming echo of my own voice, sounding with eerie mockery from round about, answered me. I listened intently. Silence, a great, brooding silence, intensified by the darkness, by the magnitude of the cavern, and by my own breathing. I no longer heard the droning sound that I had noticed when I first regained my senses, so it must either have been my imagination or the effects of the drug I had been forced to inhale. Undoubtedly I was entirely alone in the darkness. And if I were being held for ransom, it would, be only a question of time before my captors brought me something to eat and drink.

Then there was the matter of the rock camouflage. The outlaws had probably hidden one of their number beneath it as a measure of precaution in case their plans miscarried. But what an elaborate precaution, when there were so many other simpler, and equally effective, methods of concealment. And they put it in a position where it would be bound to attract attention and investigation. Even putting it behind a sotol plant would be better than having it in the open. Could it have concealed the entrance to the cave I was now in? Then, why hadn't Olin or I noticed the spot when we made camp? Perhaps the bandits had covered the place cleverly, using the false rock only as a screen for exit and entrance. That might explain the sinking sensation I noticed just before the drug put me to sleep—I was probably lowered into the ground at this point. I well knew that there were countless caves in this southeastern part of New Mexico. The mighty Carlsbad Cavern itself has a great number of branching chambers that have never been explored. What could be more perfect for the purpose of kidnapping for ransom than a well-concealed entrance to an unknown cavern in this rugged, little-traveled country? In many places near the Carlsbad Cavern the roof has fallen in, leaving deep depressions in the ground; in fact, the natural entrance to this cavern is in one of such depressions. The more I thought this over, the more I became convinced that my captors had cunningly concealed a comparatively small entrance to their own private cave, and that we, unfortunately happening to camp close by, provided easy prey for their first attempt.

HOW they could have made the place look like ordinary flat ground, with no footprints or other signs of disturbance anywhere, puzzled me greatly. Several of them had come out and had seized me from behind, but how had they covered their tracks, and where had they hidden that I did not see them as I gazed around? They must have come from some distance off, and been lightning quick to get me as they did. And having captured me so neatly and noiselessly, why was I now left alone with my thoughts, free to blunder around and break my neck in the darkness? They evidently thought to cow me, so that I would prove tractable, using the terror that comes from darkness and solitude as their trump card. I resolved that, come what might, I would never let them believe that I felt the slightest fear. And I further resolved that once I was free, I would leave no stone unturned to seek out this rendezvous and capture the whole gang, if it took half the United States army. Why I have not done this will be made evident as I continue.

Just as I had thoroughly determined to make bravery my one inflexible gesture, no matter what they did to me, I became aware of a presence approaching. It was only the faintest sort of rustling sound, as though someone in a flapping kimono and sandals were walking toward me. That someone, or something, was coming toward me in absolute darkness, apparently moving at a steady pace in spite of that fact, made my bravery dissolve into thin air. After all, what is fear? We can steel ourselves to meet known dangers philosophically, or even unknown ones if they are not totally unexpected; but when we are suddenly confronted with the unknown, with all its potentialities of horror aggravated by the awful cloak of inky darkness, or any equally terrifying circumstance, we become as frightened children. It is only natural. As the rustling sound grew louder, I involuntarily uttered a stifled, sobbing moan, and sought to crawl away in the opposite direction. I found that I could not move. I was paralyzed with a blind, unreasoning, sickening fear. I felt faint with nausea, and my teeth clicked together, as though I were perishing with cold. I have said before that I have no "nerves" and that ordinary perils have never ovecome me; but this was no ordinary situation, and what I had already been through paved the way to this climax of complete terror. I felt that death, sudden and painless, would be the most welcome thing that could happen.

Whatever it was, stopped near me and I could hear it breathing faintly. I tried desperately to control the clacking of my teeth and the trembling of my limbs. I cursed myself for having called Olin, for the noise, no doubt, had attracted the creature's attention. As I could see nothing, not even the faintest indication of glowing eyes, my terror-stricken mind finally grasped the fact that no beast was near me; it was probably only one of my captors. Yet, how had he found his way to me, and where had he come from. My terror died away as quickly as it had come, leaving me still trembling and faint, but with my mind alert for what might follow, no matter how strange.

A RUSTLING sound close to my head and something touched me on the shoulder. It was a hand, bony, long-fingered, powerful, that seized my shoulder and pulled me up to a sitting position.

"Drink!" said a voice close to my ear. "Put your hands before your face, and take the bowl that is offered you." The voice had a peculiar rasping quality, as if the speaker were having difficulty in controlling his tongue, and the pronunciation of the words was done in a sort of guttural drawl.

"What is it you offer me to drink?" I asked my unseen visitor, in the bravest voice I could muster, "and why have I been brought here?"

The hand on my shoulder slowly tightened until I winced with pain. Against my lips was pressed the rim of a rough, earthen bowl filled with some cold liquid.

"Drink!" again said the voice, and I sensed the menace in the metallic, rasping words, "to struggle is useless, for you cannot see in the dark. Do as you are told, or you shall be pinioned and forcibly made to drink. The liquid will not harm you, if that is why you are fearful."

The pain from his tremendous grip on my shoulder was too much. It would indeed be of no avail to struggle in the dark with an unknown, powerful adversary who was apparently thoroughly indifferent to the lack of light. There was nothing to do but drink, and hope that he told the truth in saying no harm lay therein. It was only a small bowl, holding little more than an ordinary glass, and I quaffed the whole potion in large gulps. It tasted no different than ordinary water.

"That is better," came the voice, as the bowl was taken from me and the hand on my shoulder removed, "now I shall talk to you. Sit quite still. You cannot possibly escape, and besides I can see you perfectly, so—"

I gave a gasp of incredulity. It was conceivable that the owner of this voice might be so used to the dark that he could make his way around; but as for seeing me perfectly in this smothering blackness . . . the man must be mad! That was it! I had been captured by some lunatic, and brought to this underground cavern for a terrible purpose. My only chance was to humor the creature, to use my wits and watch for a chance to overpower him. He was evidently endowed with a sort of sixth sense, and I would have to bide my time. Then, his voice—it was not the voice of a normal human being.

"I see that you do not believe my statement," went on that drawling, peculiar voice. "You think that it is not possible for anyone to see in the dark. You not only think I am lying, but you think I am crazy. When I get done talking to you, it will be surprising if you do not think yourself crazy instead. We know no difference between light and dark, such as you dwellers on the Earth. Light is used by us only to intensify that which we already see—it is similar to what magnification would be to you. Light makes a reaction on certain nerves of ours, corresponding to your optic nerves, that simply intensifies the image. The stronger the light, the larger the image. As I look at you now, you are your normal size. We have lived and worked so long here that we are even more partial to dark than to light, although in our work we find it necessary—"

"Just a minute," I broke in, realizing now that there was indeed a dangerous madman on my hands, and that only if I pretended to keep up a discussion on the topic which obsessed him could I hope to gain his good graces, "you must remember that I have only just arrived, and know nothing about you or your work. Where are the others who are associated with you? Did you bring me here to help you in any way? I'll be glad to do anything I can."

"I am not sure you will be needed after all," said the voice, "I am appointed to look after you until—well, until you are summoned. The others you will see in due time. Meanwhile, as you have that human trait of curiosity and your face has expressed bewilderment and incredulity at certain things I have said, I shall explain what and who I am, so that you will grasp what I am talking about. To begin with, I am not a human being. Do not, however, let that fact alarm you. Because you cannot see me, and because I am talking to you in a language you can understand, you think I am utterly insane. You will shortly see for yourself that I am right. Listen carefully to what I tell you, so that you will be prepared to comprehend what will be shown you later."

"But if you are not a human being," I expostulated in a bewildered tone of voice that I strove to make matter of fact, "what are you? You speak English very well, and only human beings can talk. Are you a god of some sort?" I thought by this remark to flatter the fellow, and thus draw him out further in his absurd statements.

"Foolish one, of course I am not a god. But your question is reasonable, nevertheless. You suppose that only human beings can talk, which is correct as far as it applies to inhabitants of this planet. My parents came from the planet you know as Venus about one hundred of your years ago, and I myself was born here, in this cavern!"

AT this amazing statement I must have registered a very ludicrous astonishment, for my invisible captor gave a deep, throaty laugh and continued: "It is too bad you cannot see yourself now, Mister Stan-lee Murduck (that is about the way he pronounced it). You, too, would laugh. You see, we are not without a sense of humor. I know your head is seething with a conflicting tumult of thoughts. How did I know your name? From the notebook you had in your shirt pocket. You would no doubt be interested in my name. It is Oomlag-Tharnar-Illnag, or Oomlag for short. You may call me that. I am sorry that I cannot let you see my face just now, but we prepare all our involuntary visitors with a little talk in the dark first, so that our intentions will be made clear and they can better stand the shock of seeing us and our work."

"Do you mean to tell me that other people have been brought here, too?" I shuddered at the thought. "What do you want with us—with me—and what becomes of us—'involuntary visitors'?"

Again came the gurgling laugh.

"Oh, we have a certain very definite purpose with you. We would not trouble to bring you here, unless we could make good use of your services. We have only invited a very few visitors, but they are all people of much more than ordinary intelligence, such as yourself, and peculiarly fitted to aid us in our—ah, purpose."

I realized fully my terrible position—talking in black darkness with a madman who claimed that his parents came from Venus, that others were associated with him in some sinister undertaking here in the cavern, and that several other people had also been made prisoners, for what unholy purposes I could not guess. The darkness and the strength of my unwelcome host were against me. In despair, I was now certain that my only hope was to draw him out in "a little talk," and perhaps thereby gain information to help me escape, or, by pretending to be very eager to help him, to insinuate myself into his good graces and catch him unaware at a favorable moment.

"YOU tell me," I said, as casually as possible, "that your visitors are allowed to see your work, but that before that event you prepare them by a little explanatory lecture here in the dark to better withstand the 'shock.' Would it be presumptuous of me to ask why it should be a shock to see you and your work?"

"Not at all," came the voice of Oomlag. "But before I do that, you should be enlightened further as to why you are here. In a way, you are our slave, in the sense at least, that you will be compelled by us to spend the next few years underground. However, if you cooperate with us as I believe you will, you will be well treated and allowed to roam around as you please. If, after things have been fully explained to you, you do not prove agreeable and refuse to help, I can only say that you will very soon change your mind.

"Now, if you will be kind enough not to interrupt me, I shall give you a little discourse that you will probably not believe. No matter. You have all, being earth creatures, been most skeptical about what is, to your way of thinking, impossible. But at least try to follow me, and when you *do* see us at work, you will be less apt to think it is all a dream or that you have lost your reason.

"As I said before, we are from the planet you call Venus. For many hundreds of years past we have been in a high state of civilization, one as far superior to yours as yours is to that of the crudest cave-man. We have developed certain scientific instruments and discovered forces that enable us to do things scarcely dreamed of by your scientists. Some of these things you will be shown in due time. It is well that we have made the wonderful advance that we have, for it has given us the secret of interplanetary flight, and in time to relieve the pressure of our population. Fortunately, your earth is only a little larger than ours, some 10%, and though almost half again as far away from the sun, your atmosphere is even better suited to us than our own. It is cooler and more stimulating. We were energetic enough as it was, but here on your earth we are paragons of energy. After we have conquered you and eventually exterminated you, as all your own superior tribes have done to your own inferior ones, we shall be the absolute masters of the two planets. With what we already know, plus things we shall find out as we begin to expand, I know that our population problem will not bother us again for untold centuries.

"After we have consolidated our position here, we intend to make an expedition to the ruddy planet you call Mars. We do not intend to settle, as conditions are not at all favorable for prolonged life there for us; but we do intend to see that the Martian civilization is broken and we ourselves secure from their menace. Though we cannot live comfortably on their planet, they can on yours, so it is wise to crush them as soon as possible, as they have a rather advanced civilization and might outdo us later. As for the larger planets known to you, such as Saturn, Neptune, and Uranus, and our smaller neighbor, Mercury, they may be disregarded, some being populated by crude insect-like creatures and others having only a low form of vegetation. Besides, their mass alone would prohibit our survival, even as it would yours. Though I weigh several pounds more here on your Earth than I would on Venus, its only effect is to give a corresponding feeling of well-being. Those who have come here direct, as my parents, say it is like a man under weight getting his full quota of flesh; he feels stronger, and he is stronger."

THE creature paused, and I could hear his garments rustling. In spite of the fact that I still thought I was dealing with a lunatic, I felt but little fear. Though the strange throaty quality of his voice gave the words an accent rather difficult to understand at times, his choice of English was excellent and stamped him as a man with a splendid education. Perhaps he was some professor of astronomy who had become insane from overstudy, and was living his life underground, clever enough to wrest a living by going at times to the outside world and obtaining food somehow. Long familiarity with his habitat undoubtedly explained his uncanny ability to get around in the dark, and sense my position. And his rock camouflage—that was wonderfully clever. Yes, I would rather deal with an intelligent man obsessed on one subject than with a rambling, mumbling idiot. Could there be any truth about others working with him? Hardly. Later he would probably point out an imaginary series of tunnels and what not, firmly believing everything was there. If I was diplomatic enough I might get him to show me the entrance through which he had brought me, and then make a break for freedom. . . .

My face must have betrayed my growing interest and lack of fear, for Oomlag's next remark indicated as much.

"What do you say now, Stan-lee?" he asked me, his garments still rustling like strips of dry, hard leather rubbing against each other. "Have I told you enough to make you realize how very much you are in my power, and to make you wish to see the things I have mentioned; or do you wish to ask questions about things I have overlooked? Our Field General has communicated with me, wanting to know if you are sufficiently enlightened. If you care to proceed now, I shall give the signal and we may advance; but if you are still afraid for your safety, further parley is your privilege."

My mind was made up. Under the circumstances, there was only one thing I could do—go with the fellow, and find out once for all whether he was a lunatic or not. I could only hope I would not be hurled into some pit in the darkness.

"Sure, Oomlag," I said, striving to seem very enthusiastic, "bring on your big show! Tell your General I am ready, and that my services are at his disposal. I think I can stand about any shock now."

"You stood the darkness test better than most," remarked Oomlag, dryly. "Usually we must speak long before we get near enough to touch. The fluid you drank was water with a mild drug to make your mind more active. Since you are ready, I will give the signal."

Again his garments rustled. About a minute passed, but nothing happened to break the impenetrable darkness or my keyed-up sense of suspense.

"The Field General says to bring you in. Stand up, Stan-lee!" Oomlag ordered, at the same time grasping my right elbow with his lean, powerful fingers. As soon as I was on my feet, he faced me half way around and gave me a little shove.

"Walk straight forward until I tell you to stop!" he commanded, the gruff, guttural words being spoken close to my ear, "and do not speak a word. Say nothing until you receive my permission."

I took a few slow, shuffling steps into the darkness, hands held before my face.

"Walk naturally!" Oomlag whispered, and there was nothing to do but obey. The floor of the cave sloped gently down, and I expected momentarily to go hurtling into some chasm. I was wholly at the mercy of this strange being, and tried to steel myself for whatever might happen. I imagine that walking the plank would be a similar sensation, the only difference being the certainty of destruction.

AFTER I had taken about a hundred steps, the floor seemed to become level. Oomlag was right behind me. I could hear the soft shuffle of his feet and rustle of his clothes. But he gave me no more spoken directions. Either I happened to be going in the right direction, or, what was more probable, I was being guided by some unknown influence. The floor continued level, and we must have walked fully five minutes in the dense blackness of the place before I noticed a little draft of warm air. At the same time I became aware of a rather high-pitched humming sound that grew louder as we moved forward. Then I began to hear more shuffling sounds, and a sort of subdued murmuring on all sides, as though a crowd of people were gathered and whispering to one another.

Suddenly Oomlag's hand grasped my shoulder and stopped me in my tracks. Without uttering a word, we stood there, his hand still gripping my shoulder. My senses were keenly acute, and I knew, from the indistinct rustlings and murmurings I could hear, that we were surrounded by other beings.

Slowly, as the lights in a theater are gradually turned on, objects around me became visible. First I could make out several shadowy, tall figures standing about on all sides, and the outlines of two enormous white stalagmites. As the light became brighter by imperceptible degrees, I could see that it emanated from a multitude of octagonal crystals set in the walls of the cavern at regular intervals. Before me rose up a sort of throne built into a large niche in the cavern wall, and on this throne, apparently hewn from the living rock, sat one of the most preposterous-looking beings the imagination of man could conceive. The two stalagmites flanked this throne on either side, and other bizarre creatures were thronged in the space between the stalagmites and below the throne.

I shall do my best to describe the Field General commanding the hordes from Venus that are to conquer our earth in a few short years. I was sickened by the revelation that Oomlag was indeed no madman, but really one of an invincible vanguard with the world in their grasp. The Field General, as Oomlag had termed him, was a terrible thing to look upon. A tall figure, well over seven feet, with unbelievably long, skinny arms and legs, a torso like a pouter-pigeon, and above it, set on a short, thick neck, a head shaped like an ostrich egg. The head was entirely bald, covered with skin like parchment and of a most revolting ochre yellow color. The ears tapered almost to a point; the eyes, small and set close together, burned like those of a cat in the dark; the nose was very wide and flat, almost pig-like; and the mouth, thick-lipped and exceedingly wide, was doubly hideous due to the total absence of chin. In conversation later he revealed his teeth, the front four evidently filed to a point and the rest flat; all of a dark gray color. He was clothed in some sort of tight-fitting dull green garment which, together with a brick-red jacket or vest over his huge, round chest, gave him the appearance of a grotesque turnip. On his long, tapering feet he wore flat sandals held in place by thongs laced through the ends of his doublet, if I may call it that. His fingers were all long and of equal length, and he kept toying with some object resting in his lap. It looked like a bassoon without the mouthpiece.

THE lights had now reached their maximum, giving the huge room the effect of being flooded by intensely bright moonlight. Behind me, and on all sides, stood scores of these creatures, similar in appearance to the Field General on the throne, except that they wore dull green jackets instead of brick-red. They stood motionless, regarding me stolidly with their smoldering, beady eyes.

Oomlag stepped forward and saluted his commander with a sweeping motion of his right arm. He said something in a strange, guttural tongue, and the Field General evidently plied him with questions about me, for they kept up a long conversation, often glancing my way. Finally Oomlag turned to me.

"The Field General wants to ask you a few questions," he said, stepping to one side.

The Field General regarded me intently for several moments. I quailed under the inspection of those calculating, cat-like, inhuman eyes of his. The only difference between him and what might be imagined in a nightmare was that he was the real thing—actual and horrible to look upon. With his loose, ochre lips exposing the sharp front teeth at every word, he spoke in a pronounced guttural accent, his English quite limited and hard to understand.

"You work rock work?" he asked with difficulty.

"Yes, sir," I replied, my heart pounding against my ribs for all I could do to calm myself. "I'm a geologist."

A short interjection by Oomlag evidently explained to the Field General what a geologist was.

"You know then what is r-r-radium?"

"Yes."

"You know what is bismuth?"

"Yes."

"You know any in between?"

"What do you mean by that, sir?" I inquired.

The Field General spoke a few rapid words to Oomlag, who said to me: "He means, do you know of any element of atomic weight between bismuth and radium? You know, of course, they are roughly 208 and 225, using 16 for oxygen as the standard, and I promise you, on my word, that if you can place any element in that gap, you will be well rewarded for the information."

"There has been none discovered that I know of," I replied.

"That is all," said the Field General, curtly, adding something in his own tongue to Oomlag.

Again came the high-pitched humming sound, and the lights dimmed perceptibly. The creatures round about, who had regarded me stolidly during my short conversation with the Field General, now broke up into little groups of four or five and walked off in different directions.

From this large room, which was the executive chamber of the Field General, branched four tunnels, about twenty feet in height and the same in width, lighted at intervals of some hundred feet by octagonal globes, set in niches in the solid rock and projecting out at an angle of 45 degrees. Down one of these tunnels Oomlag now bade me walk, himself striding along beside me, like some over-fantastic figure in a parade of mummers. We had only gone a short distance from where the tunnel branched from the Executive Chamber when I noticed that on both sides appeared, at regular intervals, large curtains or hangings of material resembling the jackets these people wore, both in color and material.

"These hangings," said Oomlag, in the same way a guide would point out and explain objects of interest to a tourist, "conceal doors to our apartment houses. Our mode of life is practically the same as yours; we breathe, we take food through our mouth, we require shelter, we mate, we are gregarious. The apartments proper I am not permitted to show you, but this I can say: they are hewn from the solid rock, as are all these tunnels, by our own machine brought from Venus. As you shall probably spend several years down here with us, it is desirable that you should have this preliminary trip and explanation before you are assigned to quarters. By the way, Stan-lee—I forgot you are an earth creature and subject to more frequent pangs of hunger than we. Do you care for food or drink? It is only a short distance to the dining room of our involuntary visitors, and I shall be glad to take you there before we go further. What do you say?"

EVER since my introduction to the Executive Chamber, I had wondered, in the back of my mind, where my fellow prisoners might be. I had seen no living thing save these monstrous men of Venus, and this sounded like a chance to see some of the other unfortunate human beings held captive here.

"Yes, I am very hungry, Oomlag," I lied, "and I was just about to ask you if I could have something to eat."

"Follow me."

I followed Oomlag down this main tunnel about a quarter of a mile to where a smaller tunnel branched to the right. Some hundred paces we took down this, then found the way blocked by the usual dull-green hangings. Oomlag's hands reached under his jacket, there was a rustling sound, and instantly the hangings parted, revealing doors like huge square blocks of cement. These doors slid noiselessly into the walls of the tunnel on each side.

We entered a chamber about a hundred feet square and about fifteen feet high, containing a dozen large, round tables of smooth rock, with smaller stools, also of rock, serving as chairs. Over each table, as well as in the corners of the room, were the octagonal crystal lights illuminating the room with their cold, intense rays. Behind us the immense doors slid together again without a sound.

At one of these rock tables Oomlag and I seated ourselves. Again he reached under his jacket and again there was a rustling sound. I was about to ask him what sort of signals he produced by this mysterious maneuver, when a panel in the rock wall at the far end of the room slid back, and a girl bearing a tray stepped out.

Needless to say, I regarded with extreme interest this first person of my own race I was privileged to see, who was, like myself, a captive of these terribly efficient Venusians. Was it sympathy with her plight that made me think her pretty? She seemed of a Spanish type, her long black hair parted smoothly in the middle, and hanging in glossy braids on either side of her pale, pathetically piquant face. She was clad in a dress made of the universal material used by these people, reaching almost to her ankles. Though she was small, the garment gave her a look of height and dignity. She moved gracefully to our table, and without a word placed before us the dishes on her tray. As she leaned over, she glanced at me with such a hopeless look in her large, brown eyes that I was stabbed to the heart. Before she turned away, I saw a tear rolling down her cheek. She brushed at it with a slender little hand, as she retired with the empty tray through the rock panel, which closed silently behind her.

"That," said Oomlag, arranging the dishes before me, "is one of our most valuable guests. She has been with us almost five years, and has been invaluable in teaching us Spanish and English. She came from a small town in Arizona. I forgot to tell you, you are to hold no converse at any time with any of your fellow beings. To do so will have painful consequences. You think she is pretty, don't you?"

I boiled inwardly. This leering, inhuman brute was my absolute master, and nothing I could say or do would help in the least; on the contrary, if I said what I really thought, it would be the worse for me.

"Oh, she's not so much," I said, casually. "She is too pale, for one thing. Tell me, Oomlag, what is this dinner you have ordered for me? How do you grow anything fit to eat down here? What is this soup made of?"

Before me, in hollow stone dishes, was a repast of hot soup, vegetables and bread. The only utensil was a large spoon made of some sort of fibre.

"While you eat," said Oomlag, stretching his long legs and adjusting his jacket, "I shall endeavor to explain things to you. Before I can answer your questions, it is necessary to trace out certain other things. Take your soup and tell me what you think of it."

I did so, finding it very delicious, rather like mock turtle. I told him it was very palatable.

"I am glad you like it. It is a combination of crushed yucca roots and prairie dog bones, prepared according to our own formula."

I made a wry face and laid the spoon down.

"Ah, I see your imagination tells you the soup is not so good." Oomlag grinned horribly, his yellow lips baring his sharp teeth. "Strange how you creatures allow your imagination to dictate your likes and dislikes. If I had not told you the ingredients of that soup, you would have enjoyed it thoroughly. Now, having told you, you find it disagreeable, though you just finished saying it was good. You might as well learn to like it, for you will have it every day. The vegetables are—but I must begin at the beginning. Not such bad bread, is it?"

"TO begin with, we are, as I told you before, from Venus. Our scientists have spent centuries in perfecting a machine for interplanetary flight. We have long had the necessary power. The problem was to determine the relative position of the two planets, the pull of gravity of the sun, Venus and your earth, the time necessary to make the flight, the provisioning and ventilating of the projectile, the perfecting of a device to detect and repel meteorites, and countless other problems, all vitally important. The data for all this was handed down from generation to generation, and finally everything had been thought of.

"No doubt you have been curious to know why the Field General interrogated you about bismuth and radium. He has had too much to do supervising things here, so has only a smattering of your languages; but that question he felt he should ask you personally. The reason is, we have an element about half-way in the atomic scale between bismuth and radium which gives us unlimited power by the breaking up of its atoms. We know that this element does exist on this earth, and the Field General thought perhaps you knew of its discovery. That, however, is only incidental, and not the reason for bringing you here.

"Having found out how to harness this element, we were well supplied with light and power on our planet. These lights you see are run by radio current from several plants in our workings, each dynamo, if I may call it that, generating a powerful radio wave which is caught and utilized by each of these crystals. The crystals are considerably larger the further away they are from the source of power, for distance demands more filament to catch the power waves.

"A fortunate discovery, though with tragic consequences to the discoverer, revealed the possibility of utilizing this element with another in such proportions as to repel anything in front of the wave generated by their intermixing. That was the beginning of our centuries of work on an interplanetary machine. It is obvious that if the ray generated by these two elements will repel anything in its path, then by proper control, intensifying and reducing it at will, enough force could be made to repel us away from Venus and toward the earth, using auxiliary rays to repel any stray meteorites. And there are plenty of those. But the exhaustive calculations! Nothing could be left to chance. The best brains of our people worked ceaselessly on the problem until everything was figured out.

"I do not think it is of much use to try to explain to you the workings of the interplanetary machine, since you are unfamiliar with the element responsible for its success. All I can say is, each of the two combining elements are kept in finely powdered form in separate containers negative to their power as lead is to your X-ray. The proper amount of each to be combined is let carefully into a tubular apparatus, separated by a thin sheet of negative metal which is then withdrawn by a special device. The power wave produced by the resulting combination is carefully calculated, and the charge is renewed in another tube at just the right moment. A battery of auxiliary tubes is always kept here for any unexpected occurrence which might take place at any moment.

"My parents told me that the take-off was most exciting. Countless thousands of my fellow Venusians were crowded as close as they could get to obtain a last glimpse of the travelers. At exactly the right moment, the big projectile soared slowly into the sky, gradually gaining momentum as it left the stratosphere and entered outer space. Faster and faster it went, with its meteorite detector busily at work spotting and repelling these menaces, and its tubes taking larger and larger quantities of the precious elements. You can judge for yourself the speed they attained when I tell you it took exactly six of your months for my people to get here."

"Pardon the interruption," I said, munching a piece of the bread that tasted exactly like a dry waffle, "but how did you know where you were going to land? Suppose you had dropped into the ocean, or even in the midst of a populated district? How and why did you hit this part of New Mexico?"

"That is explained by the atomic telescope, an invention of my great-great-grandfather's. Using the element similar to radium as a base, we wash a sensitive plate with this certain mixture containing a large proportion of that element. In order to save time, let us call this element 'Venusite' which, though not the name we have for it, is more descriptive and makes it easier for you to understand. This telescope is tremendously long, and contains a series of condensing reflectors of such accuracy and delicacy that when it is trained on a certain spot, an image on your earth, 30,000,000 miles away, is recorded on an inconceivably small part of the sensitive plate. This plate is then treated by an agent which causes the atoms in the 'Venusite' to start breaking up, and as they do so, an enlarged image is thrown on a screen. By exposing various parts of the sensitive plate in rapid succession, a series of images is obtained. We thus succeeded in exploring the surface of your earth thoroughly, proving to our own satisfaction that we could not only live on your planet, but live better than on our own. We saw that this region was practically uninhabited, and had the advantage of possessing enormous caverns suitable for housing us. It remained only to calculate the proper time for leaving in order to hit this spot. A slight error put my people several hundred miles west of here, but by a skillful handling of the 'Venusite' they managed to bring their machine down by the entrance of a huge limestone cave. The rest was easy."

DURING the latter part of this conversation I noticed that Oomlag reached under his jacket several times and made the funny rustling sounds I had heard before. I asked him what he was doing.

"Oh, yes, our portable wireless, by means of which we can communicate with anyone else in the workings."

He unbuttoned his jacket, exposing a contrivance about 18 inches square at the base, with a dome-like top, suspended from his shoulders and held in place by a strap around his waist. This explained the pouter-pigeon appearance of these people. Several slits about half an inch wide radiated from the center of the dome, and from these slits little flashes of light darted with bewildering rapidity. Several little knobs or buttons protruded from all sides of the square base, and these Oomlag was manipulating with his long, tapering, yellow fingers. As each button was pressed, it gave out a slight, crackling sound.

"This wireless apparatus," continued Oomlag, pressing a button which caused the little flashes to cease, "is extremely simple. The case is constructed of a metal much lighter than your aluminum, and in it is housed a certain proportion of our indispensable 'Venusite,' in containers unaffected by its action. These buttons on the right release certain proportions of 'Venusite,' which send out a power wave depending in intensity on the mixture. Other buttons cut off the wave, so that messages can readily be sent in code. The buttons on the left are used to tune in on incoming messages. Important messages are assigned to a certain wavelength, controlled by one button which is always plugged in; others merely vibrate, and as each individual has his own code call, no attention is paid to other messages unless the individual gets his code call. The vibration of the apparatus against our chest is all we need to understand incoming messages. You would be surprised at the lightness of these vibrations. If you had the thing on, you would probably not notice them at all."

By this time I had finished my meal, and I must confess that I enjoyed it exceedingly. I had not dared to ask Oomlag what the vegetables were, after learning the composition of the soup. They tasted like cauliflower and artichoke.

Oomlag, seeing that I had finished, manipulated a button on his wireless set, and in a moment the girl appeared to remove the dishes.

I regarded her closely. She had been crying bitterly, for her eyes were red and swollen. As she leaned past me to pick up the soup dish, one of her soft dark braids brushed my cheek and fell into my lap. She reached swiftly down to toss the offending braid over her shoulder, and as her little hand hovered for an instant over mine, I felt a small pellet of paper drop into my open palm. Taking advantage of the fact that she was momentarily between me and Oomlag, I slipped the paper into my trousers pocket. Silently she placed the empty dishes on her tray and, without looking at me, turned and walked swiftly out of the room through the rock-panel door.

Oomlag had buttoned up his jacket and was regarding me with an expression, as it seemed, of amused contempt.

"You people think you are wonderfully civilized!" he rasped, rolling his loose, ochre lips back into a revolting grimace. "Yet you are at the mercy of any number of tiny germs. You kill each other, at the slightest provocation. What forces you know about, you do not yet know how to handle adequately. What wonderful, dumb slaves you will make for us!"

HE leaned forward, his cold, glittering, pupil-less eyes close to mine.

"August 21, 1931! Remember that date. Our system of underground tunnels will then be perfected, our power bases established, the charges of 'Venusite' in place and ready to be set off. Under each of your largest cities even now work is being carried on. On that date the 'Venusite' under these cities will send its destructive wave rolling upward, and the centers of the cities will be ground into dust. In the midst of this confusion our lieutenants will emerge and assume command. Anyone resisting will be instantly destroyed by 'Venusite' guns. Nothing in the world can withstand us, and the way will be paved for our complete mastery of your earth. Slaves you will be, among other things preparing for us a certain alloy of metals common here, scarce on Venus. In a little while we shall have sent enough of this back to

Venus to bring thousands here. It is only a matter of time before your race will be entirely supplanted by ours. It is the law of Nature."

He stopped and looked at me with an expression of fiendish, smug self-satisfaction. His horrible words made me quail inwardly, but I determined to show a disinterested calmness, a scientific detachment suitable to one in my profession.

"If you are so smart and powerful," I said, boldly, "why did you find it necessary to live all these years underground? Why didn't you simply stay on the surface and sweep all opposition before you without bothering about these tunnels and charges you mention? I'm rather inclined to think it is all a big bluff, and your 'Venusite' not what it is cracked up to be. You've proved it is powerful, all right, but there wouldn't be enough of it to do all the things you say. You couldn't possibly make such a series of tunnels in such a few years."

I paused for breath. Oomlag was busy manipulating his wireless contraption. He grinned at me sardonically.

"Show me!" I continued, vehemently. "There is one thing we humans pride ourselves on, and that is our sense of logic. It isn't logical that you could do all these things. You are here, fighting for a toe-hold on our planet, afraid to come out in the open and fight. Why? Because you have just barely managed to get here, and now find yourselves isolated with no means of retreat, and unable to advance. You are . . ."

I stopped, caught by the malevolent expression in Oomlag's eyes. He had ceased to handle his wireless and his devilish grin had changed to a look of cold hatred. He leaned forward, and for a moment I feared it was his intention to throttle me. I realized that I had gone too far with my bold talk; but just as I was steeling myself for the feel of his terrible fingers around my throat, his ochre lips revealed his pointed teeth and he threw back his head with a guttural laugh.

"Your sense of logic! It is well that the humor of your remarks struck me, for I might otherwise have choked you into insensibility." His fingers drummed lightly on the table as he continued.

"Let me warn you, my friend, never again to talk that way to me or any other of us. We lose our tempers easily, especially when a slave addresses his master as you have done. But you are new here and I shall overlook it this time.

"A fine sense of logic you must have! Seeing what you have, knowing what you do, to think that we would be at the end of our rope! Do you think for an instant that we would come here, and then be unable to return to Venus or defend ourselves? Why, we have sufficient 'Venusite' to do our work here for twenty years more, destroy any feeble resistance you might offer, and send the projectile back to Venus with the alloy needed to construct hundreds more. What a fool you are, you poor earth creature! And among your fellows you are accounted wise!"

I WAS too elated that his change of mood had saved me from the consequences of my foolish remarks to feel any resentment at his description of my mental prowess. I grinned a sickly grin, and said nothing.

Oomlag rose to his feet.

"Come!" he said, shortly. "We have wasted enough time. I had intended to take you elsewhere first, but now I shall give you a glimpse of our space projectile. There is also another thing I wish to demonstrate to you, after which you will be assigned to quarters. Your duties will be explained later."

Again the doors slid back and we were once more in the large hallway. We proceeded down this perhaps a half mile, passing many of the Venusians hurrying back and forth, emerging from and disappearing behind the hangings on each side. They all regarded me curiously, but without hostility. I was surprised at the lack of conversation. Many had their wireless sets crackling, but none spoke to each other or to Oomlag. I surmised that this hallway was the main residence section, and that the creatures we passed were temporarily off duty.

We stopped before a large curtain covering an enormous section of the left wall. Oomlag gave a short signal with his wireless, the curtain parted, the usual stone doors slid silently open, and we entered a tremendous, brilliantly lighted room. In fact, this room was so much more brightly illuminated than the hallway, that it took me several seconds to adjust my eyes to the glare. As I stood there, blinking, Oomlag spoke a few low words to a huge Venusian who, I noticed, held in each hand a long, cylindrical object like that which the Field General had been toying with.

As I grew accustomed to the unusual brilliance, I took in the details of this astounding cavernous chamber. It must have been at least five hundred feet across, perfectly circular, and evidently hewn from a natural cave, for hundreds of feet above me gleamed the points of scores of large stalactites. Around the sides of the room, placed at intervals of about ten feet, were round objects about the size of basketballs. In the exact center of this mammoth cavern rested a huge, octagonal contraption with a rounded top that I knew must be the interplanetary projectile itself.

Oomlag tapped me on the shoulder.

"Stan-lee," he said, grinning horribly, "you are now privileged to inspect the masterpiece of our civilization—the space flyer in which we came from Venus to your earth. Much of what I will show you will baffle your intelligence, but it will give you an idea of how powerful we are. This machine serves now as our central power plant. See those tubes projecting from the sides? Half of them are supplying power to those round transformers you see, which in turn transmit the invisible energy to the lights in the various rooms and hallways nearby. Other power stations are scattered through the workings, supplying the laborers with the light which increases their efficiency and the power to drill the tunnels. You would be surprised at the number of your big cities which are already undermined and ready for the day in which we strike. I told you when that would be: August 21, 1931. On that day our kinsmen on Venus will carefully observe your earth, and will witness the well-timed explosions. They will see us emerge; they will see— but enough of that! Come! I will show you the inside of the machine."

AS we approached this huge contrivance, I marveled at the smoothness and symmetry of its surface. It must have been at least eighty feet in height by thirty in width, a perfect octagon to within about fifteen feet of the top, which was dome-shaped. It was constructed of something that looked like highly polished gun metal. At regular intervals from the sides projected short tubes arranged in clusters of eight, which Oomlag had said were the power tubes; these, however, were the only visible break in the shining surface of the machine. I wondered how we were to enter the thing.

That question was soon answered. The big Venusian who had admitted us to the room, and who apparently was the sole guardian of this valuable chamber with its vital apparatus, stepped ahead of us and pointed one of the round objects he carried at the side of the flyer. Instantly two doors flew out, making an opening about four feet wide and six feet high into the projectile. Stooping, Oomlag entered, and I followed close behind him. Without a sound, the doors shut behind us. At last I was actually inside the wonderful space flyer that had brought this vanguard of horrible, super-intelligent beings to conquer our helpless earth! With hardly controlled excitement and curiosity I gazed around.

We were standing in a brilliantly lighted octagonal chamber some twenty-five feet across, with a metallic ceiling about twelve feet from the floor. In the center of this ceiling was a circular opening about six feet in diameter through which extended a round, perpendicular shaft like the slide pole in a fire station. On each side, opposite the walls of the chamber, were tall metal devices, for all the world like elongated hour glasses, extending from floor to ceiling. On the neck of each was an intricate series of valves and pipes, and from the base of each "hour glass" innumerable small tubes led to the walls. Although I couldn't hear a sound, I seemed to be conscious of a sort of vibration that made me sense the powerful forces that were at work. At the base of the pole in the center was a round platform which, as I looked, slid noiselessly out of sight up the pole, descending in a few seconds with a couple of Venusians. These, after a curious glance at me, busied themselves inspecting the machinery, reading dials, and moving various handles on the different valves.

Oomlag had been watching me with smug satisfaction, evidently deriving much amusement from my open-mouthed expression of amazement.

"Yes, I thought you would be entertained by this little visit," he chuckled. "Gaze upon the highest development of our genius. Simply by making a change in the amount of 'Venusite' introduced into what you might call the condensing tubes, the power generated is controlled. You already know the power of 'Venusite' when you realize that it brought us from our planet to yours; you can imagine, then, what very minute quantities are needed to supply power.

"These tubes leading from the base of these generators carry the concentrated power impulses to the tubes you saw on the outside of the flyer. These in turn bombard the round objects you saw placed near the walls of the room, which operate to diffuse the power beam in various directions through the workings.

"The wall of this chamber is an inner partition, giving a vacuum protection against the cold of outer space. Before I go any further, it is necessary to show you the upper compartments of the flyer, where we store the reserve supply of 'Venusite' and have the living quarters of the travelers. We have a very clever arrangement for preparing concentrated foods. The capacity of the flyer——"

OOMLAG stopped. The door of the projectile had opened, and the big Venusian guard had entered and broken in abruptly on Oomlag's talk. He spoke a few rapid, guttural words to my guide, while the door meantime remained open.

Oomlag scowled, and seemed to be considering what he had just heard. He cast a glowering, sidelong glance in my direction, and I guessed that I must be concerned in some way. Finally, he said something curtly to the guard, and faced me. I was relieved to see his face light up into a grin which, though evil and hideous, was a grin nevertheless.

"We shall step outside a moment, Stan-lee," he said. "I have some important news for you which should make you feel pretty good."

Wondering what he could possibly mean by this, I followed Oomlag and the guard out of the flyer into the intense light of the large cavern. As soon as the doors had swung shut behind us, Oomlag spoke.

"The Field General has commanded that you be released!"

I gasped with amazement. Surely, there must be some mistake! Released, knowing what I did about their plans, free to take steps to stamp out this menace, to——

"Stan-lee, I see you are incredulous. Nevertheless, you are to be released, immediately." Oomlag came closer, leering into my face. "The Field General has a sense of humor, just as we all have. It is really our one weakness. He feels your presence here is undesirable, and your services are not needed after all. That leaves two alternatives—either kill you, or let you go. He has decided on the latter. Myself, I am sorry, for I have taken a liking to you."

I was stunned. Like a fool I blurted out:

"But—but, you have shown me—how do you dare——"

"I know what you think." Oomlag spoke suavely, mockingly. "You think that, once free, you will spread the alarm to your fellows. How ridiculous! In the first place, no one would believe you, you would be considered mad. In the second place, you humans could do nothing to hinder us if you wished. We have the power of 'Venusite.' I need say no more. It is one of the best jokes I ever heard! You alone of the earth inhabitants will know of our existence, and your knowledge will be useless. You can do nothing, absolutely nothing. Your friends will discover you, wandering. A word of this to anyone—well, your mind has been wandering, too!"

I was sickened by his fiendish, throaty laughter as he derided me, mocked me with this terrible truth.

Suddenly his manner changed. The leer on his face was replaced by an ugly snarl of determination. He uttered a few words in his own language, and I felt myself seized from behind. Oomlag's ochre face came close to mine.

"Goodbye, earth creature. You go out the way you came!"

Again I felt myself blindfolded and gagged, rapidly losing consciousness under the influence of the sweetish drug . . .

The rest can be told in a few words. I regained consciousness not far from the camp-site. The sun was high in the heavens. I staggered to where I had seen the rock camouflage. It was not there—absolutely no sign of any disturbance, nothing but ordinary flat ground. Something made me think of the note I had received from the dark-haired girl. I found it where I had stuffed it in my pocket. In a hasty scrawl she had written, in charcoal, now scarcely legible:

"India is safe."

The sun was setting when Olin appeared with a posse in search of me. I trumped up an explanation of how I had been restless, had gone for a ride in the moonlight, had been thrown from the horse . . . what else could I do? It was as Oomlag had said.

Now, in India, I write these lines. The girl must have thought I had a chance to get free. My friends, for God's sake do not regard me as a second Jack Pansay with his phantom "rickshaw."* Olin knows I disappeared—and I know what happened. If I am not spared to read this document myself, for the sake of those who *will* believe, give it circulation. How wise was Shakespeare when he had Hamlet say: "There are more things in Heaven and earth . . ."

I can say no more.

THE END

Milton Keynes UK
Ingram Content Group UK Ltd.
UKHW030744071024
449371UK00006B/571